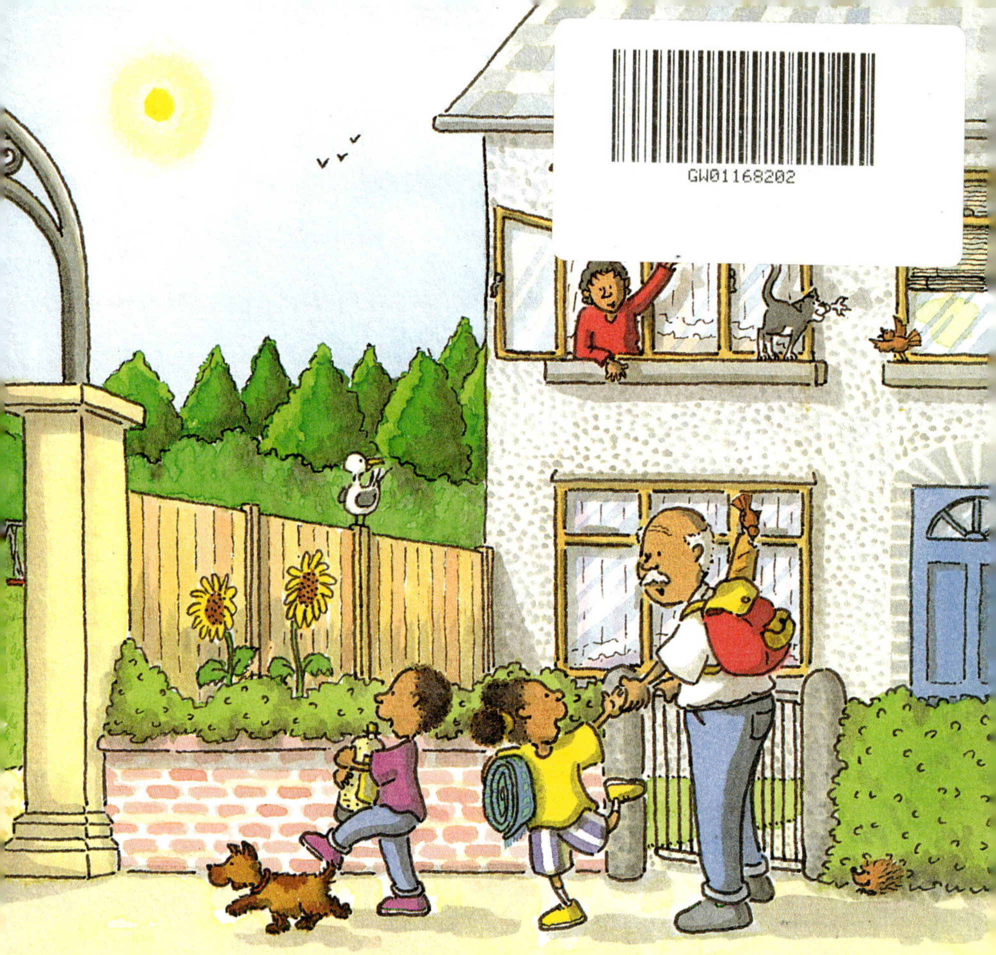

We're going on a picnic.

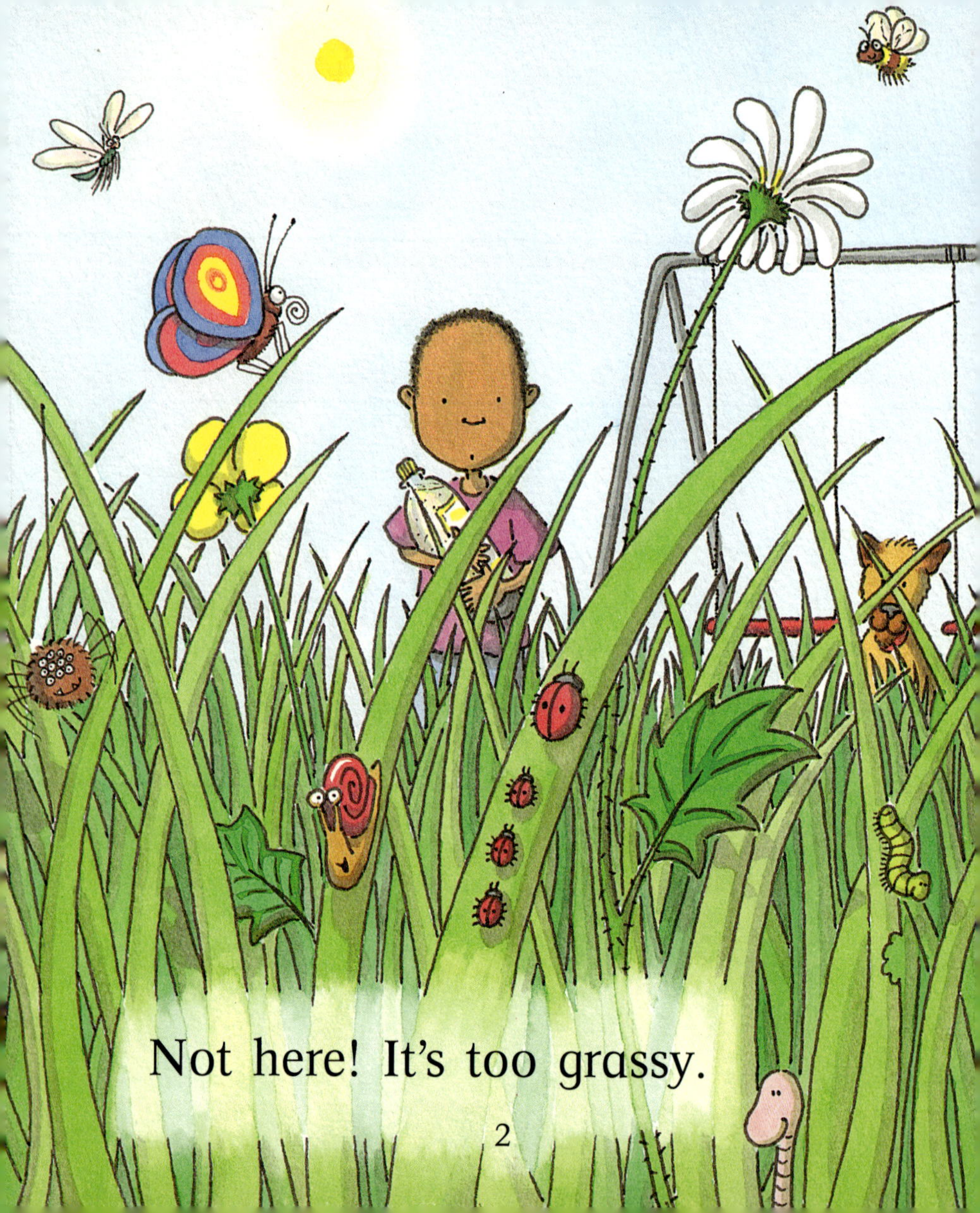

Not here! It's too grassy.

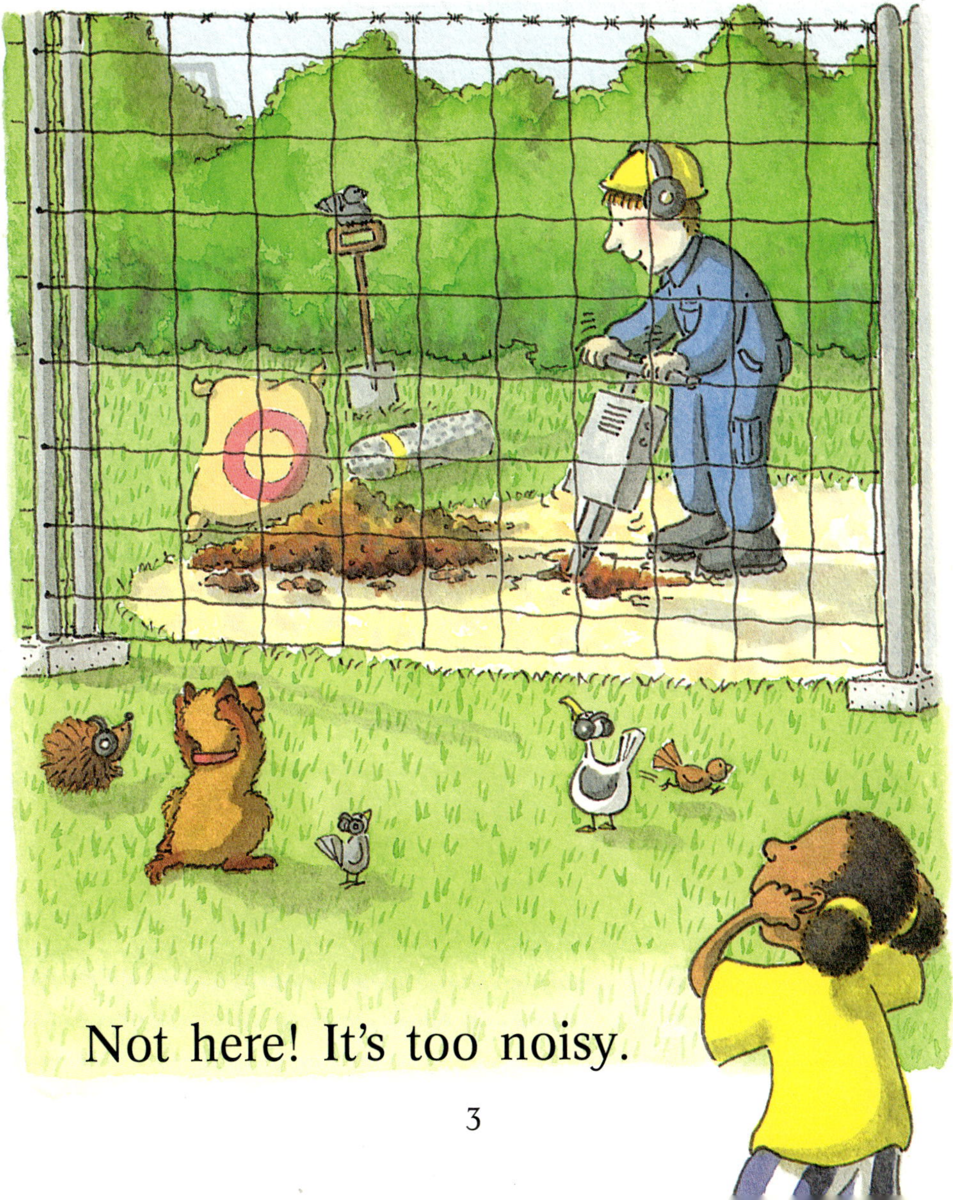

Not here! It’s too noisy.

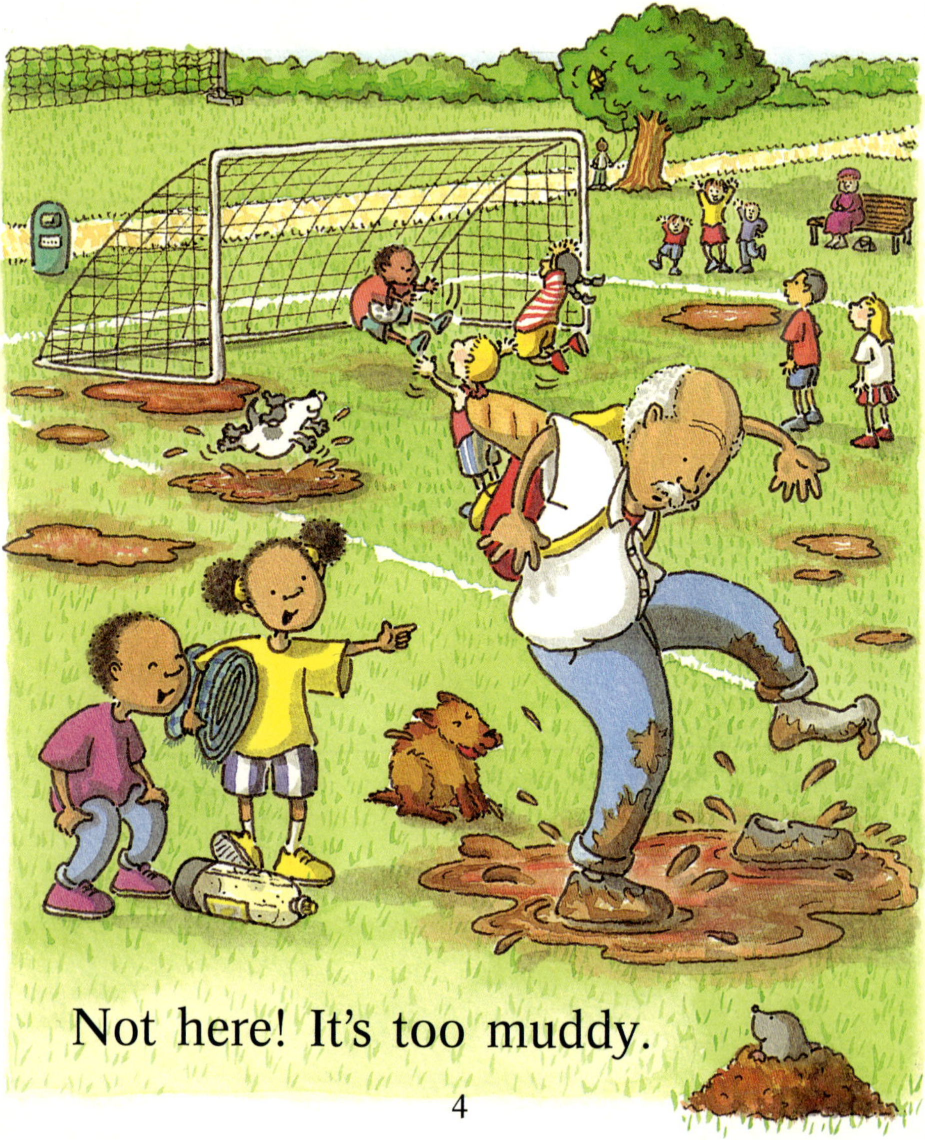

Not here! It's too muddy.

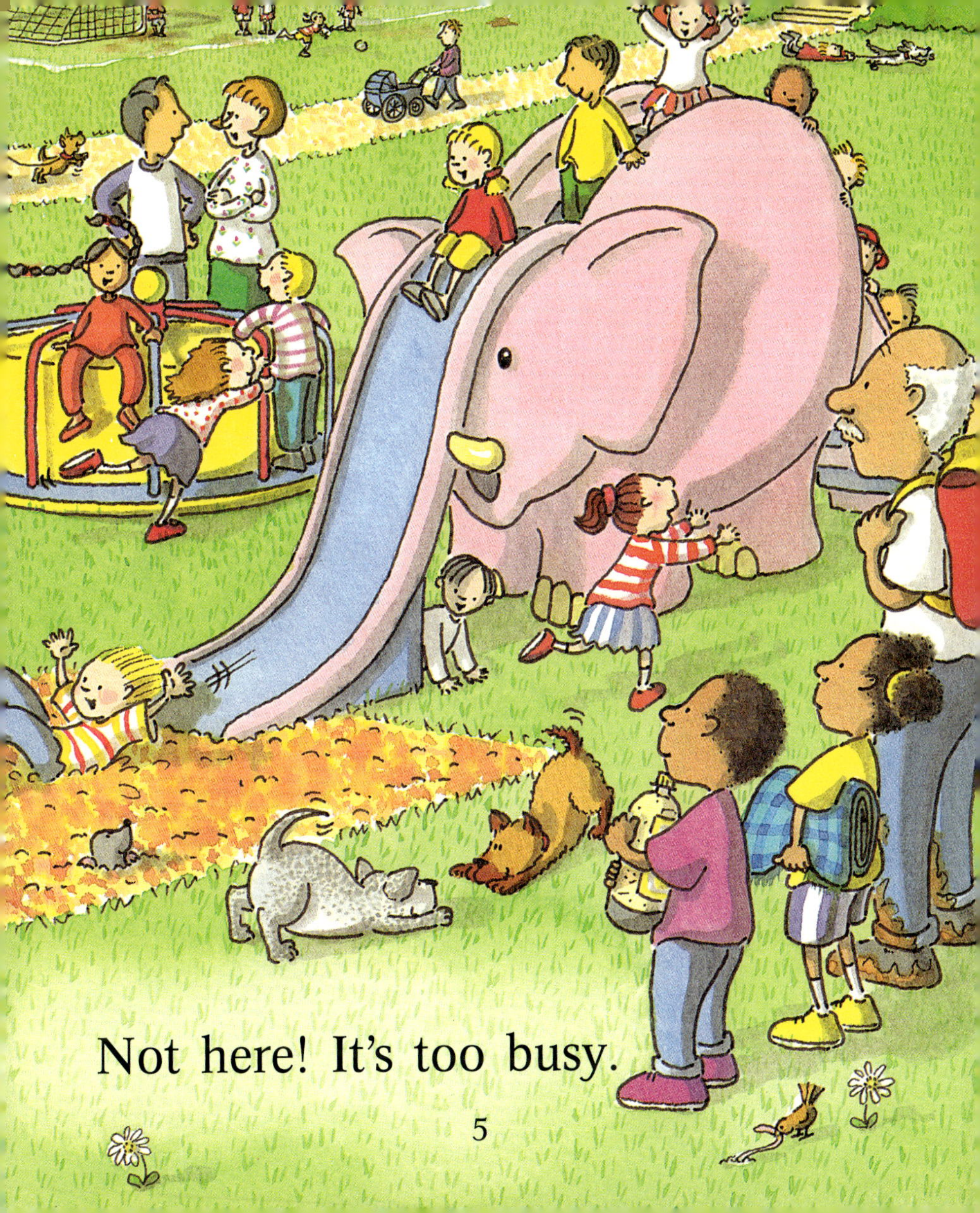

Not here! It's too busy.

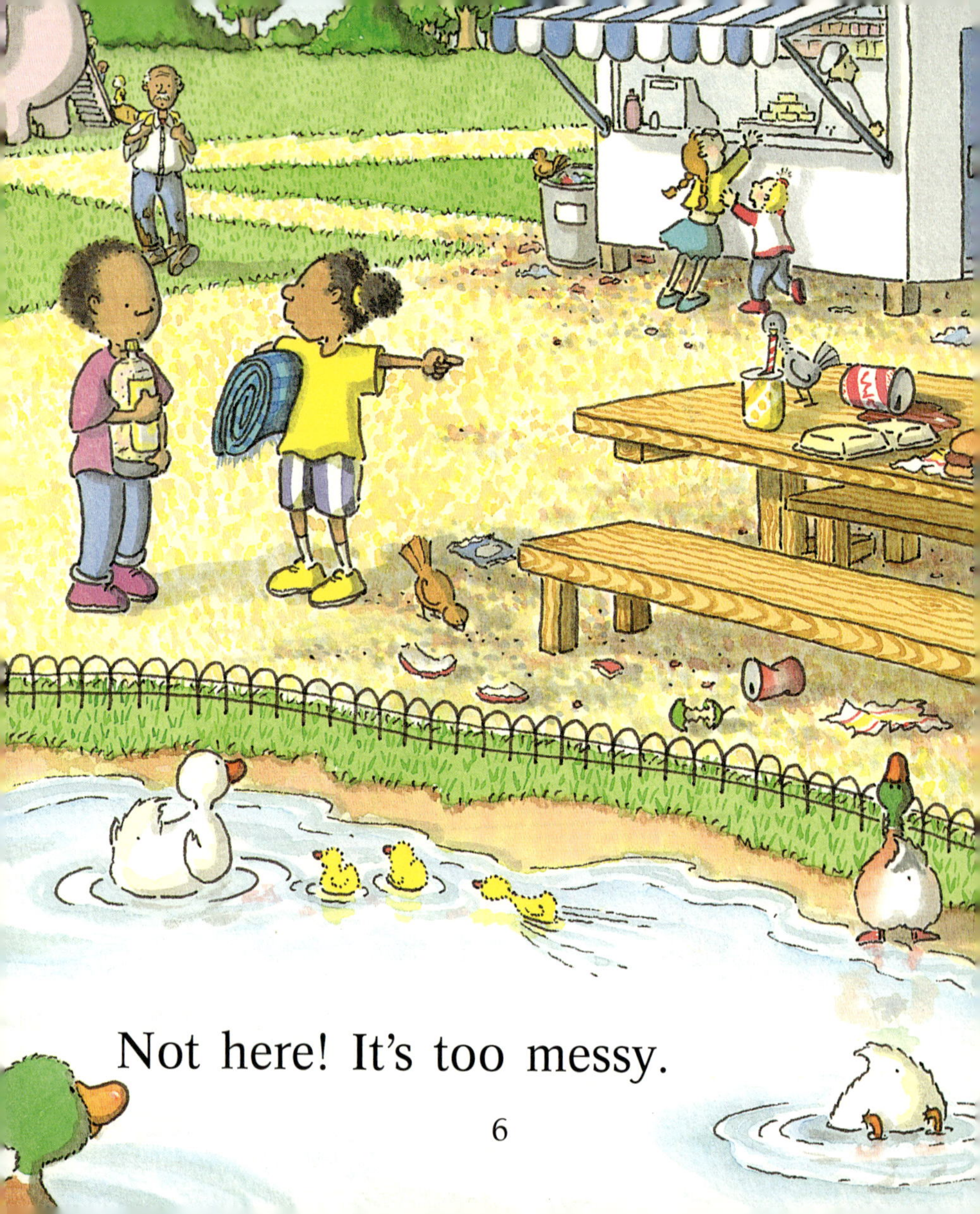

Not here! It's too messy.

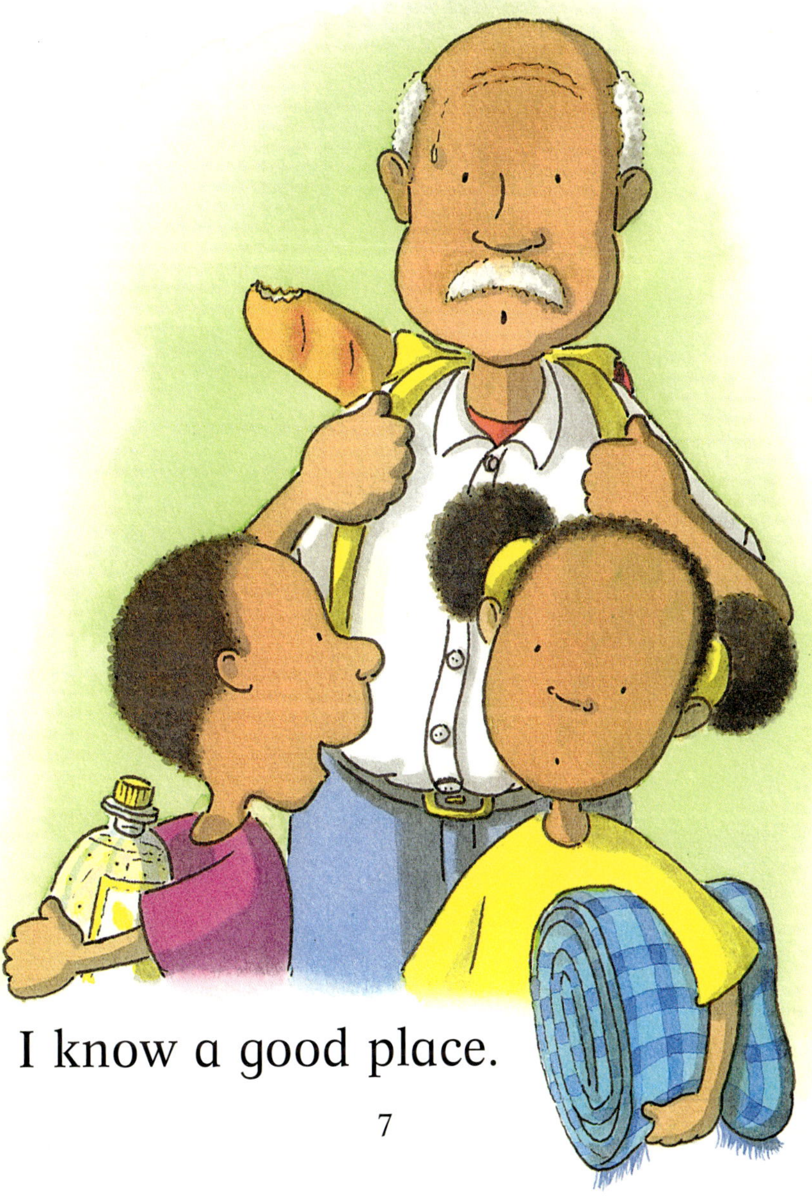

I know a good place.

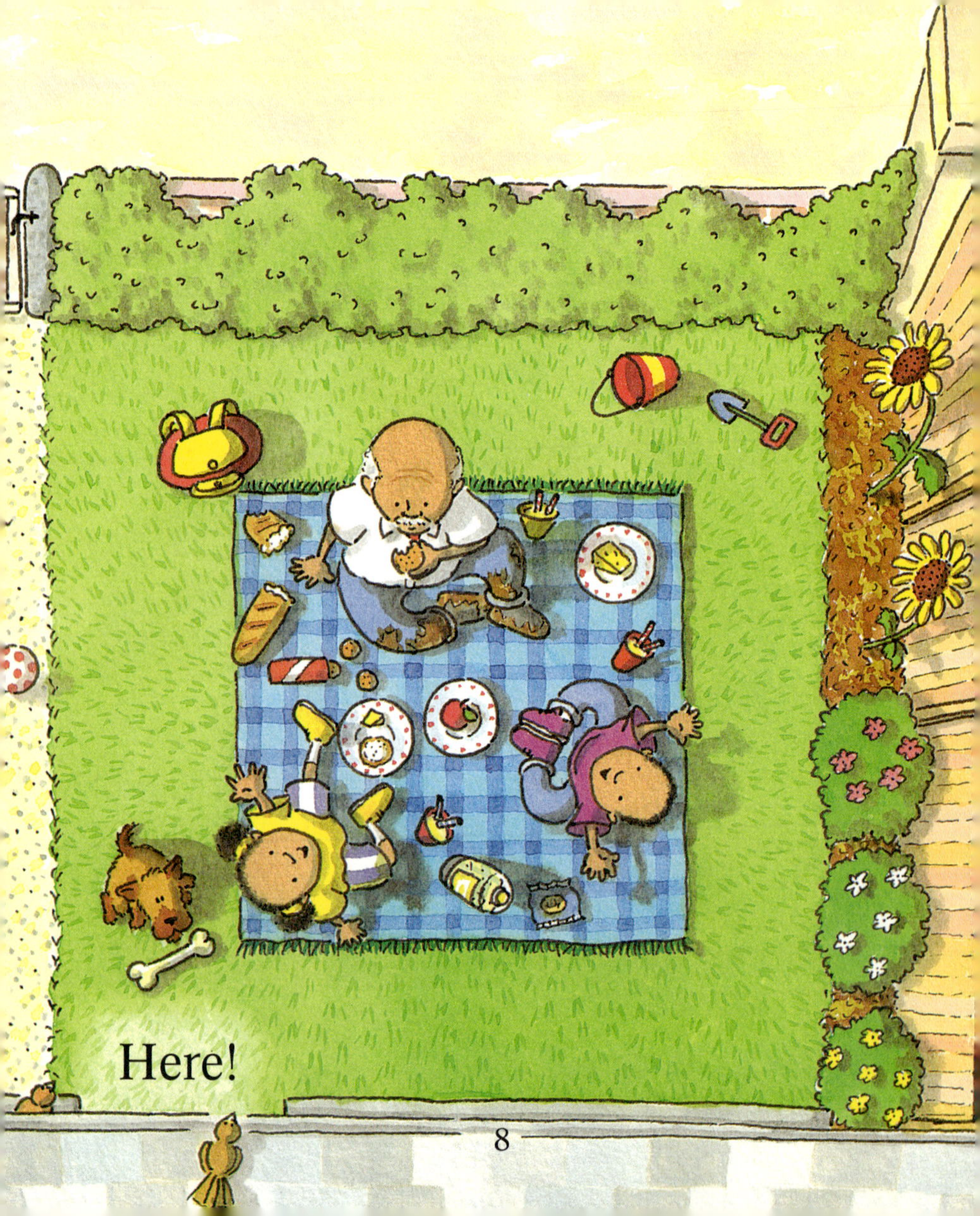

Here!